OUR VOICES

SPANISH AND LATINO FIGURES OF AMERICAN HISTORY™

JOAQUÍN MURRIETA

ROBIN HOOD OF THE CALIFORNIA GOLD RUSH

AVERY ELIZABETH HURT

rosen publishing's
**rosen
central**

New York

Published in 2020 by The Rosen Publishing Group, Inc.
29 East 21st Street, New York, NY 10010

Library of Congress Cataloging-in-Publication Data

Names: Hurt, Avery Elizabeth, author.
Title: Joaquín Murrieta : Robin Hood of the California Gold Rush / Avery Elizabeth Hurt.
Description: First edition. | New York : Rosen Publishing, 2020. | Series: Our Voices: Spanish and Latino Figures of American History | Includes bibliographical references and index. | Audience: Grades 5–8.
Identifiers: LCCN 2018007102 | ISBN 9781508184843 (library bound) | ISBN 9781508184836 (pbk.)
Subjects: LCSH: Murieta, Joaquín, –1853—Juvenile literature. | Revolutionaries—California—Biography—Juvenile literature. | Mexicans—California—Biography—Juvenile literature. | Outlaws—California—Biography—Juvenile literature. | Frontier and pioneer life—California—Juvenile literature. | California—Gold discoveries—Juvenile literature. | California—History—1850–1950—Juvenile literature. | California—History—1846–1850—Juvenile literature.
Classification: LCC F865.M96 H87 2019 | DDC 979.4/04092 [B]—dc23
LC record available at https://lccn.loc.gov/2018007102

Manufactured in the United States of America

On the cover: Joaquín Murrieta (1829–1853) was a hero and freedom fighter to his fellow Latinos and bandit and scourge of the gold rush to US authorities.

CONTENTS

INTRODUCTION

A poor Mexican family is struggling to get by. They live in California during the gold rush of the 1850s. But gold hasn't been rushing their way lately. They tried to stake a claim in the gold fields, but the white settlers chased them off. Then they moved into a shack on the land of a cousin who farms, but he's not doing too well either. The farming hasn't been good, there's not enough to eat, and now one of the children has taken ill. Times are hard.

Then one day, the family returns from the fields to their tiny cabin to find a burlap bag sitting right in the middle of the rickety old dinner table. Inside the bag are medicines for la chiquita and enough money to buy a week's worth of groceries.

Murrieta has been by!

Many stories like this one have been told about Joaquín Murrieta. He was a bandit and leader of the outlaw gang known as the Five Joaquíns. He was said to be like the English Robin Hood or "Pretty Boy" Floyd of Oklahoma during the Great Depression, stealing from the rich and giving the money to the poor. He punished the wicked and helped the people who had been treated cruelly or unfairly.

Yet Murrieta is a mysterious figure. There are plenty of stories about him, but few facts. He was born in Mexico, in the state of Sonora. According to most of the stories about him, he went to California in 1849, during the gold rush, to make his fortune. Instead, he encountered vicious racism and was chased out of the mining camps. After that, the stories say, Murrieta turned to

Joaquín Murrieta, 1829–1853

a life of crime. He and a gang of bandits stole horses, attacked wagon trains, stole from the passengers, and killed many people.

However, not everyone says he was wicked—or at least not totally wicked. Many, many stories tell of him helping the poor and the suffering. So who was Murrieta, really? Are the stories about him true? Was he a hero? Or a dangerous outlaw? Or maybe a little bit of each?

No one really knows for sure. It's often that way with legendary heroes. When hard facts about a person's life are elusive, sometimes people make up stories to fill in the details. And those stories often make these heroes into whatever people need them to be at the time. If they do some good at a time when some good is really needed, people might overlook their bad deeds and celebrate the good ones. If they are really evil, it's convenient to forget that even very bad people often have some good in them.

The whole truth about Murrieta will likely remain a mystery forever. But the few known facts and stories are decidedly exciting and fun. Get ready to learn what is known, what remains shrouded in uncertainty, and what historians and history enthusiasts like to believe about the man who came to be known as the Mexican Robin Hood.

CHAPTER ONE

"THERE'S GOLD IN THEM THAR HILLS"

I t was January of 1848, and James Marshall was building a sawmill on the American River in the Sacramento Valley of California. He happened to glance down and see something shiny in the water below. He took a closer look, and sure enough, it was gold.

A POPULATION BOOM

Marshall scooped up a handful of the gold nuggets and showed them to his partner, John Sutter. Sutter wanted to keep the find a secret, but soon other people began to find nuggets of gold in the American. Even then, most people didn't believe it. Gold floating in the river—free for the taking—seemed too good to be true.

Samuel Brannan owned a store nearby. Brannan didn't expect to make a fortune panning for gold.

At Sutter's Mill, California, in 1849, James Marshall spied a glimmer in the water: so began the gold rush.

He had other ideas. He knew that he could make a lot of money selling supplies to people looking for gold. Brannan started telling everyone he saw that there was gold in the river. Word spread quickly, and soon the news was in the papers not only in California, but as far away as New York. Still many people thought it was some kind of hoax. Then in his annual address to Congress, President James Polk mentioned that gold had been discovered in California. That was all it took. Soon people were flooding into California from the rest of the continent and even from Europe to search for gold. In 1849 alone, an estimated one hundred thousand people had rushed to California hoping to pull a fortune out of the river. They were called forty-niners.

Some people did indeed get very rich. But most did not. Before long, most of the gold that had washed into the river had been panned out. Getting gold now required mining, which was far more difficult and dangerous. Many people who traveled to California to look for gold lived in mining camps. These were makeshift towns built quickly just for the miners. Life in the camps was very difficult. Some people lived in rough shacks, others in tents. The camps were rough and lawless places. In 1851, Louise Clapp wrote a letter to her sister, describing the mining town where Clapp and her husband lived. She said even the doctor's office had a dirt floor. There wasn't much to eat. Fruits and vegetables were scarce. Eggs and bread were extremely expensive. Many miners became ill and malnourished.

BUT WE WERE HERE FIRST

Life during the gold rush was especially hard for Mexicans. Mexicans had lived in California since the 1700s—long before Anglos had settled there. Mexico had gained independence

OCCUPATION FOR RAINY DAYS. A PLEASANT SURPRISE.

SCENES AT THE GOLD DIGGINGS.

On the page herewith we present five pictures so expressive and characteristic, that but few words are required by way of explanation. The series tell a connected story at a glance. The first picture represents the manner in which the gold diggers of California are accustomed to occupy themselves on a rainy day, viz., in mending their clothes, and repairing their boots and tools —in-door occupation, and a very necessary duty. The second picture is rather a ludicrous one, and represents an interior view of a man's cabin, which has been taken possession of by one of the numerous bears that abound in the diggings, and which seeming to have regaled itself sufficiently on the stores of the cabin is now seen warming itself, after the style of a human being across a chair. The third, and centre picture, is a very fine and expressive one, representing the miners engaged in weighing the dust which has cost them so much labor to procure. The tools of their calling are strewn upon the table before them, eating utensils, firearms and scales. One is enjoying his pipe, and another looks on thoughtfully at the operation of weighing performed by his comrade. The fourth picture, below, represents the miners engaged in performing their culinary duty. One is actively engaged over the fire, with the food, the savory smell of which attracts the dog hard by, who eyes it wishfully, while the other miner is pounding up corn with a pestle and mortar, to make a pudding with which to finish the meal. Hunger is said to be the best sauce for sup-

per, and consequently, as these hardy sons of toil have plenty of appetite, we must suppose that their sauce is of the choicest sort. The fifth and last picture, represents the miners washing their clothing on the river's bank, and hanging the clothes to dry on the branches of the trees. Their wants are simple and easily supplied. They require neither starching nor ironing for their coarse under clothes, and they are quickly cleansed and ready for use without the laundress's care. To many this life, aside from the

idea of profit by the obtaining of gold, has its charms; and we must confess that we do not wonder that a feeling of this character should possess many a stout heart and gallant spirit. The very flower of New England youth—that is to say, its bone and sinew—have emigrated to the shores of the Pacific, in search of the shining metal and of adventure. As we have before taken occasion to remark, there are very few families, even, who do not count one or more members of their circle as among the gold seekers and California adventurers. The consequence of this immense amount of manual labor devoted to the purpose of mining, is to increase both the yield of gold and the mortality of the country, which, to a vast number of constitutions, proves fatal. And while some return enriched with gold, to the scenes of their childhood, a vast number die at a distance from friends and home.— Many philosophize and say that the discovery of gold in California is, in reality, a curse rather than a blessing. They adduce all the contingent evils that have resulted from the matter, but forget that they cannot divine the hidden purpose of Divine Providence, that has thus revealed the hidden wealth of the earth to men's eyes. The ways of Providence are inscrutable, and no man can fathom them. But that the discovery of gold in California and Australia savors of some goodly use be-yond its apparent application, we have not the shadow of a doubt. It seems to have been reserved till this day, as one important auxiliary in bringing the whole world under the influences of civilization and religion.

REPRESENTATION OF MINERS WEIGHING THEIR GOLD.

MINERS PREPARING THEIR FOOD. MINERS WASHING THEIR CLOTHING.

Life in the mining camps during the gold rush was often rowdy, but it was also always hard, even for the toughest miners.

from Spain in 1821. The Mexican government rewarded soldiers and people who had helped achieve independence by giving them huge tracts of land in the California Territory. Mexican citizens who lived in California were called Californios. Anglos and immigrants from Europe began to settle in the area in the 1800s. But when the gold rush started, in 1849, there were still very few of them living there.

Just a month after James Marshall saw that glint of gold in the river, the Mexican-American War ended. The United States

This 1847 map of the United States of Mexico shows the territory that was given to the United States of America in the Treaty of Guadalupe Hidalgo.

NOT JUST LATINOS

California's gold rush was hard on Mexicans and Californios. But they were not the only people to be mistreated by the many Anglos coming in to the area in search of fortune. Many immigrants from China arrived, and they were often driven from their mining claims or, worse yet, killed. After the first Foreign Miners Act was repealed, another one that specifically targeted Chinese miners replaced it. Native Americans were also victimized. They were often treated no better than animals and sometimes killed for sport. Before the gold rush, California was home to more than three hundred thousand Native Americans. Within twenty years two-thirds of them had died. Some died of diseases, others died in accidents. But thousands were murdered.

and Mexico signed the Treaty of Guadalupe Hidalgo. Because it had lost the war, Mexico agreed to give the United States a lot of territory. Some of this was land that had been given to Mexican citizens in 1821, after Mexico won its independence from Spain. When the gold rush began, hundreds of thousands of newcomers arrived. When they failed to strike it rich mining gold, some of them took over the land of the Californios who lived there. White people in the camps often mistreated Mexicans who came to California to find gold.

Mexican miners from Sonora, the home of Joaquín Murrieta, already had a lot of mining experience. They were particularly skilled at finding gold. This didn't please the hordes of Anglos coming in, who were afraid that the Mexicans would dig out all the gold before they got theirs. Sometimes when Mexicans found a good source of gold, Anglo miners would take it over, even violently, if necessary. American miners started posting signs warning that all "foreigners" had twenty-four hours to clear out of the mines, or they would be thrown out.

In 1850, at the height of the gold rush, California, which had just become a state earlier that year, passed the Foreign Miners Act. This was a tax on any non-US citizens who were mining for gold. Many Mexicans weren't able to pay the tax and had to give up mining.

After a few years, most of the gold had been discovered. When there was no more gold to dig for, many of the forty-niners turned to farming. They often took over the land that had been given to the Californios by the Mexican government. The Treaty of Hidalgo had made Mexicans living in California into US citizens. Their rights to the land should have been protected. Some people tried to prove their right to their land in court, but the process was expensive. Many of those who managed to do so had to sell out to pay their legal fees. They lost their land anyway.

Though they had been there first, soon Mexicans and Californios became the minority in the new state, and many of the Anglos came to see them as unwanted foreigners. Some people in the new state of California wanted to exterminate the entire nonwhite population. This was the situation Murrieta likely found himself in when he came to California to look for gold.

CHAPTER TWO

THE FIVE JOAQUÍNS

Much of Murrieta's life is a mystery, but researchers have managed to piece together a few basic details. The story of where he came from and what happened to him explains a lot about the legend that quickly grew up around him.

FIEBRE DEL ORO

Joaquín Murrieta was likely born in San Rafael de Alamito, a small town in Sonora, Mexico, around 1828. If Murrieta's boyhood was typical of that time and place, he learned to farm, ride and train horses, and mine for gold. He had nine *hermanos y hermanas*, brothers and sisters. When Murrieta was a young man, he fell in love with Carmen Feliz. By December of 1849, they were married. Many of Joaquín and Carmen's friends and relatives were leaving for the gold fields in California. Joaquín's brother, Jésus, caught *fiebre del oro*, gold fever. Jésus persuaded his younger brother to join him on the trip to California to search for gold. Jésus's wife remained behind in Sonora, but Carmen decided to accompany Joaquín and his brother on the adventure north. Joaquín Murrieta was still a young man—probably about twenty-one years old. Some reports say that the young Murrieta was handsome and energetic with

The giant saguaro cactus is a distinct feature of Mexico's Sonoran Desert, where Joaquín Murrieta is thought to have grown up.

long shining black hair. He was generous and well-spoken, honest and kind. It is almost certain he was not prepared for what he would encounter in the gold fields of California.

The Murrieta family's troubles began in May 1850, soon after they arrived. One story tells it this way: They were staying at Murphy's mining camp in northern California. Jésus bought a mule from some Anglo miners there. They accused him of stealing the animal. Jésus was not given a fair trial—he wasn't given much of a trial at all. The other miners knocked together an informal court, pronounced Jésus guilty, and hanged him on the spot. A few days later, twelve Anglos rode out to the place where Joaquín and Carmen had staked their claim. They assaulted then killed Carmen. They beat up Joaquín and left him for dead. But he survived!

EL PATRIO

Even if Murrieta had tried to get justice in court, he would not have been successful. At the time, it was illegal for a Mexican to testify against an Anglo in court. So Murrieta took justice into his own hands. He began to hunt down and kill the men who had committed these horrible crimes. Murrieta may have wanted revenge only on those who had murdered his wife and brother, but things soon got out of hand. In a very short time, he found himself the leader of an outlaw band. The gang included five men named Joaquín. In addition to Joaquín Murrieta, there were Joaquín Botellier, Joaquín Carrillo, Joaquín Ocomorenia, and Joaquín Valenzuela. They became known as the Five Joaquíns, and soon were notorious enough that almost any crime or murder would be put down to them. They were accused of carrying out a series of crimes. They were said to have robbed banks, rustled cattle, and, according to some records, murdered dozens of people.

So how did this man who was thought to have killed so many people come to be a hero?

Mexicans and Californios were treated very poorly by the Anglos who were flooding into the area where they had lived for so long. It was easy for them to seize upon the story of a man who had been brutally treated and was now out for revenge. Murrieta's personal story quickly became a symbol for a larger pattern of injustices. Rather than a wicked murderer and hooligan, Murrieta came to be seen as a resistance fighter, struggling against imperialism. He didn't become a hero because he killed people or even because he got revenge on those who had killed his family. He became a hero because he was seen as someone who stood up to those who oppressed his fellow Latinos. Americans called him a *bandito*. Mexicans called him *El Patrio* ("The Native")—another way of saying, "he is one of us."

EL ZORRO!

The first American superhero was Latino. In 1919—years before Superman or Batman arrived on the scene—writer Johnston McCulley created a character called *El Zorro* ("the fox" in Spanish). Zorro was incredibly dashing. He wore a black cape, a black mask, and rode a black horse named Tornado. He fought his enemies with a sword. Of course, he always won. Zorro did not have any superpowers, but he was extremely clever. He often outwitted his opponents and left them looking foolish and humiliated. He operated in California in the period just before the gold rush, defending the poor and the powerless against their oppressors. In the very first Zorro story, the black-caped avenger confronts an enemy. "I am a friend of the oppressed," Zorro says, "and I have come to punish you."

Historians believe that Zorro was based on none other than Joaquín Murrieta. If that is the case, then Murrieta was the inspiration for an entire American superhero tradition. Bob Kane, the man who created Batman, said that he based his caped avenger on Zorro.

Some experts think that all American superheroes are based in some way on Zorro— which means that they are also based on Joaquín Murrieta.

This is the legendary Zorro, as portrayed by actor Antonio Banderas in the 2005 film *The Legend of Zorro*.

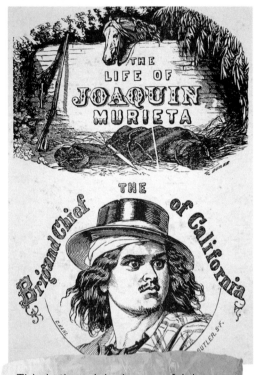

This is the original cover of John Rollins Ridge's book, *The Life of Joaquín Murieta*, published in 1859.

In 1854, John Rollins Ridge wrote a novel about Murrieta. Ridge was a journalist and based his book on newspaper articles and court records. However, he heavily embellished the story. Ridge's book describes exciting gunfights and miraculous escapes. Murrieta rescues damsels in distress and comes to the aid of the poor and downtrodden. Many similar books and stories have been written about Murrieta since. The majority of them describe him as a romantic hero rather than a *desperado*. He quickly became very much like England's Robin Hood. One book, published in 1932, is even titled *Joaquín Murrieta: The Robin Hood of El Dorado*.

Robin Hood is known for "stealing from the rich and giving to the poor." But of course, he was much more than a man in tights who redistributed England's wealth. He was revered as a leader in the resistance of the weak against the powerful in medieval England—or at least he was a symbol of that resistance. (The facts about Robin Hood are as murky as the facts about Murrieta.) Murrieta became a similar figure. Whoever Joaquín Murrieta was in real life, he has been beloved by Latinos for generations because he is a symbol of the resistance of their people to Anglo oppression.

CHAPTER THREE

BOUNTY!

If Murrieta was a hero to Latinos, he was no such thing to Anglos. On January 29, 1853, a Stockton, California, newspaper, the *San Joaquín Republican*, printed a story about the activities of Murrieta and his gang. The news report said, "During the winter months, a band of Mexican marauders have infested Calaveras county, and weekly we receive the details of dreadful murders and outrages committed in the lonely gulches and solitary outposts of that region. The farmers lost their cattle and horses, the trader's tent was pillaged, and the life of every traveler was insecure." The article went on to say that the band was led by a man named Joaquín. It did not give him a last name but did refer to him as "a very desperate man." For a time, it wasn't clear who this Joaquín was. He was a mythic figure capable of creating mayhem in several places at once. Soon the public realized that there were likely several men named Joaquín behind the crime spree. In fact, Murrieta's gang included a lot of people—not all named Joaquín. Many Mexican miners had been forced off their claims by angry Anglos. Some of them were victims of the Foreign Miners Act. Virtually all of them had been subject to a great deal of discrimination. Murrieta was not the only Mexican who felt the need for revenge.

One was a man named Manuel Garcia, also known as *Tres Dedos* ("Three Fingers"), or Three-Fingered Jack. *Tres Dedos* was thought to be Murrieta's second in command. The exact identity of Murrieta may have been murky, but everyone knew who Three-Fingered Jack was, and everyone knew he was a vicious man. He had caught the attention of the authorities some time back for torturing and killing Chinese miners and robbing and shooting Anglos.

CALL IN THE SPECIAL FORCES!

The state of California decided to put a stop to Murrieta once and for all. They offered a $1,000 bounty to anyone who brought in Murrieta—dead or alive. Of course, there was a problem with this plan. No one knew exactly what Murrieta looked like. The Anglo population was already near panic because of all the killings and reports of killings attributed to Murrieta and his gang. Since they did not know who Murrieta was, or where to find him, almost any Mexican man could be shot or captured and hanged by a mob if they thought he might be Murrieta or a member of his gang. Offering a huge reward for his capture would only make this worse. To get this under control, in May of 1853, the state legislature authorized a special force of twenty California Rangers to go after the Five Joaquíns. Captain Harry Love, a former Texas Ranger and a veteran of the Mexican-American War, was appointed leader of the group.

At first Love and his team of rangers didn't have much luck. They followed up any and all rumors about the whereabouts of the Five Joaquíns. They chased back and forth across the territory without finding even a trace of the outlaw band. Several versions of the tale have been told. In some, Murrieta and his gang break camp and leave an area only hours before the rangers arrive.

Others describe Love and his men catching up with the Five Joaquíns, only to have the outlaws make a miraculous escape. In one version, the rangers are almost ready to give up and go home when they finally come across Murrieta and his gang.

No matter what happened during the two months that the rangers searched for the Five Joaquíns, the search came to and end on July 25, 1853. The rangers found a group of Mexicans near Coalinga, California. They were camped by Cantua Creek, or Arroyo de Cantúa, as it was known then. Many of the men escaped, but rangers killed at least three of them. Two of the dead, they said, were Joaquín Murrieta and Three-Fingered Jack Garcia.

This is possibly the site near Arroyo de Cantúa where California Rangers claimed to have captured Murrieta and his right-hand man, Three-Fingered Jack Garcia.

However, to claim the bounty, the rangers had to prove that they'd killed the right men. After all, many innocent Mexicans had been killed or captured since the panic over Murrieta had taken hold. The Rangers didn't want to haul rotting corpses back to Sacramento through the summer heat. They cut off Murrieta's

HERE'S LOOKING AT YOU!

It seems weird, but it was actually very clever to put Murrieta's head (and Jack's hand) in a jar of brandy. Dead bodies don't last very long, especially in the heat. The details are more than a little gross, but basically as soon as you die, the bacteria that live in and on your body start to eat you. Pretty quickly the body becomes something nobody would want to try to identify even if they could. (According to one story, Love's men started back with the bodies, but soon realized that the corpses wouldn't last out the trip. Perhaps the odor of rotting flesh got to them.) But alcohol—like brandy—kills bacteria and dramatically slows down the process of decomposition. Even today, naturalists often preserve animal specimens in alcohol (though not brandy). Popping Murrieta's head in a jar of brandy not only made the trip far more pleasant, it really did give the authorities something to identify—if only they'd know what Murrieta looked like before he was preserved in a jar.

head and the hand of Three-Fingered Jack, placed their grisly trophies in jars, and covered them with brandy.

When the rangers reached Sacramento, they displayed their prizes. However, not everyone was convinced that Love had brought in Murrieta. (There doesn't seem to have been much

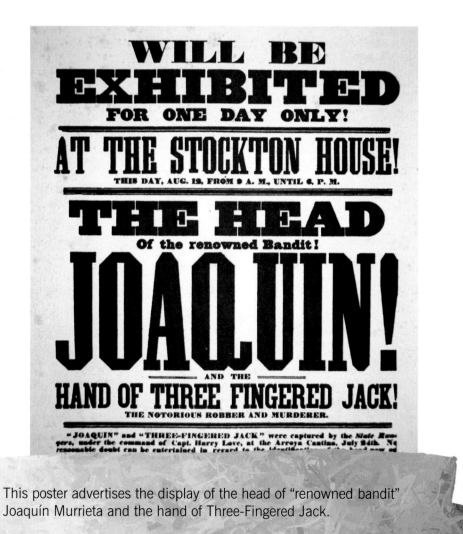

This poster advertises the display of the head of "renowned bandit" Joaquín Murrieta and the hand of Three-Fingered Jack.

controversy over Jack.) The wanted posters had described Murrieta as having dark eyes and dark hair. The man Love's men killed was described as having blue eyes and light brown, curly hair. To collect his reward, Love carried around the jar with the preserved head, showing it to people who claimed to have known, or at least seen, the famous bandit. Love managed to find quite a few people who were willing to sign a paper (or at least mark it with an X) attesting that they knew Murrieta, and this was indeed his head. This was enough to convince the authorities to pay Love the $1,000 reward.

But neither the story of Joaquín Murrieta nor of Harry Love was over yet.

CHAPTER FOUR

MISTAKEN IDENTITY?

Joaquín Murrieta and his three-fingered right-hand man had been killed and the reward paid. The story should have been over. But it was not. Many people right away doubted that Love and his men had really captured Murrieta. The Mexican community, where Murrieta was already something of a hero, refused to believe that he had been caught and killed. It was unthinkable. But it was not just an unwillingness to believe such a mythical character as Murrieta could be brought down. The *San Francisco Herald* reported that it was Joaquín Valenzuela who had been killed, not Joaquín Murrieta. Another newspaper reported that Murrieta and his men had been given shelter by Andrés Pico, a prominent Californio. It seems that the details of Murrieta's death are as murky as those of his life.

STEP RIGHT UP

Meanwhile, Love still had the head and the hand. Perhaps to supplement his reward, Love began traveling around the area charging gawkers a dollar apiece to get an eyeful of his gruesome trophy. The government may have been satisfied enough to pay Love his bounty, but the public still had doubts.

If Murrieta did retire to a ranch in Sonora, the view from his porch might have looked like this.

The general view was that Love, desperate for success and cash, had brought in a ringer—or the head of a ringer. The head in the bottle did not belong to Murrieta. The notorious outlaw was still at-large. Someone claiming to be Murrieta wrote to a local newspaper saying, "I still retain my head." Murrieta sightings became common. People claimed to have seen him in the San Fernando Valley. Others said that he had been spotted living a quiet life of retirement somewhere in Sonora.

The people who had signed papers saying that they recognized the head in the jar weren't very reliable. It was likely that none of them had ever seen Murrieta. It was likely that few people other than his friends and family had gotten a good look at him and lived to tell about it. However, while Love was touring with the head, he encountered someone who did in fact know the Robin Hood of El Dorado and knew him well. Joaquín Murrieta's sister peered in the jar and said it was definitely not her brother's head. If anyone could have made a positive ID, it was probably the sister of the deceased.

WHERE DID I LEAVE MY HEAD?

It's somehow fitting that the head in the jar came to as mysterious an end as did the man it was said to have belonged to. Love toured the area with the head for a while, but soon it seemed that everyone who wanted to see it had already done so. Or perhaps Love got tired of being on the road. In any case, the gruesome relic ended up in a saloon in San Francisco. It was kept on display there for several months but then dropped out of sight. Some said it had been stolen. Then in 1855, it turned up among the belongings of a man whose property had been seized to pay his debts. The jar supposedly containing Murrieta's head was sold at auction for thirty-six dollars.

(continued on the next page)

(continued from the previous page)

After that, it passed from hand to hand. By 1865, it was in an establishment known as Dr. Jordan's Pacific Museum of Anatomy of Science on Market Street in San Francisco. Dr. Jordan's was not nearly as scientific as the name suggests. These sorts of museums were common in those days. Their features tended more toward freak show than science. Body parts of criminals were not unusual displays.

In 1906 a massive earthquake and the fire that followed destroyed much of the city. It did not, however, destroy Dr. Jordan's. (The museum had since moved to McAllister Street in a part of the city that escaped the fire.) During the chaos, however, the jar said to contain Murrieta's head disappeared. And that should have been the end of it. But according to an article in the *San Francisco Chronicle*, a man in Santa Rosa, California, surfaced in 1970 claiming that he'd had the head all these many years. He couldn't produce it, though. Some years back he had buried it in a secret location.

This huge break in the pavement on Van Ness Avenue in San Francisco, California, was caused by the 1905 earthquake.

CHOOSE YOUR OWN ENDING

Historians who have since tried to untangle the mystery aren't sure either. Many experts doubt that the man Love killed and beheaded was Joaquín Murrieta. Some say it was indeed the head of Joaquín Valenzuela, another of the Five Joaquíns. Some think it was probably an unknown Mexican man who had the bad luck of getting caught up in the ambush. Some even suggest that Love and his men deliberately brought in the wrong man. In a version of the story retold by anthropologist Tim Christensen,

Law enforcement officers in the West during this period in history were tough customers, as tough as the outlaws they pursued.

Harry Love and his rangers seem as least as wicked as the Five Joaquíns. In this version of the tale, Love and his men were having no luck finding the outlaw band. They did not want to go back empty-handed and be branded as losers. Besides, Love wanted his reward money. When they came across a group of Mexican men peacefully camping by the creek, they saw their chance. They killed the campers and chopped off the head of one man and (after altering the fingers to make it look like Three-Fingered Jack) the hand of another. Not only had they brought in the wrong men—they had deliberately killed innocent men as stand-ins. Of course, this story is no more or less likely than any of the others. It does, however, show just how muddled the story was, even at the time

Which version of the story a person accepts may come down to what that person needs from Murrieta's story. On one hand, if you need to see Murrieta as a mythic hero, then the idea that he cleverly evaded his pursuers is very attractive. Murrieta has the last laugh and perhaps lived on to do more good and right more wrongs. On the other hand, if you need to cast him as a tragic figure—a man who meant well but was overcome in the end by greed and power—then his gruesome end is sad, but somehow fitting. And of course, if you see him as a horribly wicked villain, then it must feel good to know he got his just desserts. His head slowly rotting in a jar of brandy is a nice flourish. However, in the end, whoever he was and however he died (in a gunfight with Love or of old age on a ranch in Mexico), what matters now about Joaquín Murrieta is not who he was or wasn't, but how we tell his story.

CHAPTER FIVE

THE LEGEND

So what is to be made of the story of Joaquín Murrieta? How much of the story is true? Will anyone ever know? Can anyone ever know? And does it really matter?

THE STORY LIVES ON

Despite all the many details about his life that historians have patched together, we don't really even know if any single person ever existed who we can say is Joaquín Murrieta. Was the man who was born in Sonora in or about 1828 the same man who was the object of Harry Love's quest? Were his wife and brother really murdered? Was there a single outlaw behind all these stories, or were many acts of violence committed by many different people attributed to a single dramatic and romantic figure? The mystery of who Joaquín Murrieta was is as deep as the mystery of whose head Love put in that jar.

Murrieta's story was exciting—and became more so as the tales about him spread and were embellished. Soon after his reported death, books and stories began rolling off the presses. Rollins's famous book, *The Life and Adventures of Joaquín Murieta: The Celebrated California Bandit*, was published in

THE HEADLESS HORSEMAN OF EL DORADO

Not everyone refused to believe Murrieta was dead. Some of the stories about him involve not the surviving outlaw, but his ghost. According to a tale told in the book *The Robin Hood of El Dorado* by Walter Burns, a man named Henderson, one of the men who had brought in Murrieta's head, was for the rest of his life haunted by Murrieta's ghost. Whenever Henderson was out at dusk, a headless horseman draped in black would appear at his side and ask for his head. When Henderson protested that he no longer had Murrieta's head, the ghost would promise that Henderson would have no peace until he returned the head. In later years, Henderson would often hear a sorrowful voice that no one else could hear, saying "I am Joaquín and I want my head. Give me back my head. Give me back my head."

1854, the year after Murrieta's death. This story was obviously fictionalized; Rollins made no secret of that. The tale inspired many copycats—few of which bothered to track down the facts of the story. In one set of tales, Murrieta is moved from Mexico to Chile. The famous Chilean poet Pablo Neruda wrote a play in which Murrieta was a Chileno. Each of these works changes the story a bit here and there (or sometimes a lot). This adds to the confusion about Murrieta, but also enriches his legend. Today,

The Chilean poet Pablo Neruda, shown here in 1952, penned a play that featured a Chileno Murrieta.

more than 160 years after his death, we still know very little about Murrieta, yet his story still fascinates and inspires.

Whoever he was or wasn't in real life, Murrieta has become a legend. Legends are curious things. One way of defining a legend is to say that it is an oft-told story based on some truth. Legends spring from real people and real life, but then morph into something different and usually far more significant than the historical figure they are based on. People create legends to meet their needs. People who need a peacemaker create a legendary peacemaker. People who need an avenger create a legendary avenger.

A MAN AND A SYMBOL

Murrieta has been compared to Robin Hood, an English legend known for helping the poor and protecting the weak from the strong. But there are plenty of similar stories—many of them American. Charles "Pretty Boy" Floyd was a bank robber in Oklahoma during the Great Depression. At the time, many people were losing their jobs and having their homes taken by banks because of an economic crash that was beyond their

This mugshot is of the famous outlaw "Pretty Boy" Floyd, from when he was arrested for taking part in a bank robbery in which a police officer was killed.

control. Many stories were told about how Floyd would visit poor, struggling farmers and secretly leave behind a pile of money to help them out. Floyd became a local legend. He represented the anger of struggling farmers toward those in power whose mismanagement of the economy had cost so many innocent people their homes. Folk singer Woody Guthrie wrote a song about Floyd. One line in the song says, "You won't never see an outlaw/Drive a family from their home." People didn't approve of Floyd's violence and lawlessness, but he was a useful illustration of the many ways the structure of society itself can be violent. Driving Dust Bowl or Mexican families from their land were injustices that needed to be righted. Stories like these give people the hope of righting them.

Like these and many other legends, people remember and admire Murrieta not for who he really was and certainly not for the many crimes he committed. They tell and retell his story because he has come to be a symbol of the resistance of the poor and weak to the rich and powerful, of the ongoing resistance to racism and oppression.

GOOD GUY OR BAD GUY?

If the Murrieta described in this book is the real Murrieta, then he was definitely a criminal. He robbed and murdered and took justice into his own hands. But he was also a victim. His property was stolen and his family brutally murdered. Because of the racism of the time, he had no legal means of seeking justice. Many of his compatriots were treated in equally awful ways. For them, the Robin Hood of El Dorado embodied the rage and anger they felt about their own treatment.

This lithograph portrays a likeness of the legendary Joaquín Murrieta.

People no longer hunt down and kill their enemies. They seek justice through the courts. But even today, some people find that justice is not so easy to come by. Racism and other forms of discrimination still exist. But fortunately, other forms of resistance exist today. One can go to the polls and vote for people who will help in the struggle for justice. People write letters to our leaders to make sure they know and understand their needs. Others take to the streets to protest wrongs. Some call strikes, organize boycotts, and engage in the kind of nonviolent resistance they learned from leaders such as César Chávez and Martin Luther King Jr. We no longer resort to the violent tactics of Joaquín Murrieta. But we still look up to him as someone who did not give in to abuse. And we love to read his story and tell his tale.

TIMELINE

1821 Eleven years after the Mexican War for Independence began, the Treaty of Cordoba makes Mexico an independent nation, no longer a part of Spain.

circa 1828 Joaquín Murrieta is born, probably in Sonora, Mexico.

1846 The Mexican-American War begins.

1848 The Treaty of Guadalupe-Hidalgo ends the Mexican-American War, giving about one-third of Mexico's territory to the United States.

1848 James Marshall finds gold in the American River near Sacramento, California.

December 5, 1848 In an annual address to Congress, US president James K. Polk verifies that gold has been found in California, setting off the California gold rush.

1848–1850 The population of San Francisco, California, grows from one thousand to more than twenty thousand.

1849 Joaquín Murrieta, his wife, and brother join other forty-niners in the California gold fields.

1850 California becomes a state.

1850 The new state of California passes the Foreign Miners Act, imposing a tax on miners who are not citizens of the United States.

1851 The Foreign Miners Act is repealed.

1852 The Foreign Miners Act is reinstated with changes.

1853 (May) The California legislature forms a special force of rangers, led by Harry Love, to find and arrest, or kill, the Five Joaquíns.

1853 (July) Harry Love and his rangers bring in a head in a jar of brandy, claiming it is the head of Joaquín Murrieta.

1854 John Rollins Ridge publishes *The Life and Adventures of Joaquín Murieta: The Celebrated California Bandit*, a widely popular fictionalized account of the life and death of Murrieta.

1906 A powerful earthquake strikes San Francisco, California. In the chaos caused by the earthquake and subsequent fire, Murrieta's remains are lost.

1970 A man in Santa Rosa, California, claims to have buried Murrieta's head in a secret location. No proof of this is found.

GLOSSARY

Anglo A white, English-speaking American.

annual Taking place once each year.

brandy A strong alcoholic beverage made from wine.

compatriot A fellow citizen.

damsel A young woman, typically one in need of being rescued.

El Dorado An imaginary city of gold; a place of unusual riches or opportunity for riches.

embellish To add (usually false) details to a story to make it more interesting.

fictionalize To turn a real event or person into fiction, as in a novel or short story.

horde A crowd of people.

imperialism The practice of extending the rule of a nation by acquiring territory in other countries.

Latino A person of Latin American descent (female: Latina).

marauder Someone who roams around an area attacking people and stealing.

notorious Being famous for something bad.

novel A long fictional narrative or story.

nugget A small lump or chunk of something; often used to refer to small pieces of gold.

oppression Unfair or excessive use of authority or power.

pan To separate gold from gravel in water by gently shaking it in a pan.

revere To respect or admire.

saloon An establishment where alcoholic beverages are sold and consumed.

testify To claim under oath, as evidence in court.

villain An evil character; a person responsible for wickedness or trouble.

Autry Museum of the American West

4700 Western Heritage Way
Los Angeles, CA 90027-1462
(323) 667-2000
Website: https://theautry.org
Facebook: @AutryMuseum
Instagram: @theautry
Twitter: @TheAutry
This Los Angeles museum
is dedicated to an
inclusive exploration of the
American West.

California Historical Society

678 Mission Street
San Francisco, CA, 94105
(415) 357-1848
Email: info@callhist.org
Facebook and Instagram:
@californiahistoricalsociety
Twitter: @CAHistory
Website: https://www
.californiahistoricalsociety
.org
This is a nonprofit organization
dedicated to educating the
public about California's
history and making
that history relevant to
contemporary lives.

California Office of Historical Preservation

1725 23rd Street, Suite 100
Sacramento, CA 95816
(916) 445-7000
Email: calshpo@parks.ca.gov
Website: http://ohp.parks.ca.gov
Facebook and Twitter:
@calshpo
The California Office of
Historical Preservation
maintains and preserves
California's heritage.
Their website contains
information about historic
sites, including Sutter's Mill
and the gold rush.

Canadian Association for American Studies

Website: http://american
-studies.ca
Twitter: @CAASCanada
This multidisciplinary
organization was founded
to encourage the study of
the United States and the
implications of such studies
for Canada and other
North and South American
societies.

Gold Rush Museum
601 Lincoln Way
Auburn, CA 95603
(530) 886-4900
Website: https://www
.placer.ca.gov
/departments/facility/parks
/parks-content/museums
/gold-country-museum
Facebook and Twitter:
@placerCA
Instagram:
@placercounty
The Gold Rush Museum
features exhibits and
educational programs about
the California gold rush.

**League of United Latin
American Citizens**
1133 19th Street NW, Suite
1000
Washington, DC, 20036
(202) 833-6130
Website: https://lulac.org
Facebook: @ lulac.national.dc
Twitter and YouTube: @LULAC
This organization is dedicated
to enhancing the economic,
educational, and political
conditions and civil rights of
the Hispanic population of
the United States.

**Mexican Cultural Institute
(MCI)**
2829 16th Street NW
Washington, DC 20009
(202) 728-1628
Email: culturemexico@
instituteofmexicodc.org
Website: http://www
.instituteofmexicodc.org
Facebook: @mexculturedc
Twitter: @MexCultureDC
The MCI hosts a variety of
cultural and educational
programs.

FOR FURTHER READING

Cobb, Allen. *Mexico: A Primary Source Cultural Guide*. New York, NY: Rosen, 2004.

Fleischman, Sid. *Bandit's Moon: an Orphan, an Outlaw, and the Wild, Wild, West*. New York, NY: Greenwillow, 2008.

Gildenstein, Melanie, and Kerri O'Donnell. *A Primary Source Investigation of the Gold Rush* (Uncovering American History). New York, NY: Rosen, 2016.

Hern, Roger E. *The Spanish-American War* (Mexican America). New York, NY: Cavendish Square, 2010.

Lynette, Rachel. *The Gold Rush*. New York, NY. Power Kids Press, 2014.

Mayo, Matthew P. *Haunted Old West: Phantom Cowboys, Spirit-Filled Saloons, Mystical Mine Camps, and Spectral Indians*. Guildford, CT: Globe Pequot, 2012.

Rutter, Michael. *Myths and Mysteries of the Old West*. Lanham, MD: TwoDot, 2017.

Shoup, Kate. *The California Gold Rush* (Expanding America). New York, NY: Cavendish Square, 2016.

Shoup, Kate. *Life as a Prospector in the California Gold Rush*. New York, NY: Cavendish Square, 2017.

Thornton, Bruce. *Searching for Joaquín: Myth, Murieta, and History in California*. San Francisco, CA: Encounter, 2003.

BIBLIOGRAPHY

American Experience. "The White Man's View." PBS. Retrieved February 9, 2018. http://www.pbs.org/wgbh /americanexperience/features/goldrush-white-mans-view.

American Presidency Project. "James K. Polk: Fourth Annual Message." Washington, DC. December 5, 1848. http://www .presidency.ucsb.edu/ws/index.php?pid=29489.

Bell, Bob Boze. "Jar Head! Joaquín Murrieta vs Harry Love's Rangers." *True West*, March 13, 2015. https:// truewestmagazine.com/jar-head.

Bishop, Marlon. "Zorro: America's First Superhero." Latino USA, May 2, 2014. https://www.npr.org/2014/05/02/309020982 /zorro-americas-first-superhero.

Brenner, Erich. "Human Body Preservation: Old and New Techniques." *Journal of Anatomy*, 2014 Mar; 224(3): 316–344. https://www.ncbi.nlm.nih.gov/pmc/articles/PMC3931544.

Burns, Walter Noble. *The Robin Hood of El Dorado: The Saga of Joaquín Murrieta, Famous Outlaw of California's Gold Rush*. New York, NY: Coward-McCann, 1932.

Christensen, T. E. "The Revenge of Three-Fingered Jack." Sequoia Conservancy: Tales from the Past, January 18, 2017. http://www.sequoiaparksconservancy.org/tales-from-the-past /january-18th-2017.

Drysdale, David J. "Ridge's Joaquín Murieta: Banditry, Counterinsurgency, and Colonial Power After Guadalupe-Hildago." *Canadian Review of American Studies*, 46 no 1, 2016: 62–85.

Ejecentral. "Desmitifican Historia de Quien Inspiro Creation de el Zorro." Eje Central, November 2, 2014. http://www.ejecentral .com.mx/desmitifican-historia-de-quien-inspiro-creacion-de -el-zorro.

Griswold del Castillo, Richard. "Joaquín Murrieta: The Many Lives of a Legend." In *With Badges and Bullets: Lawmen and*

Outlaws in the Old West, edited by Richard W. Etulain and Glenda Riley. Golden, CO: Fulcrum, 1999.

Kamiya, Gary. "When an Outlaw's Severed Head Went on Tour in SF." *San Francisco Chronicle*, October 13, 2017. http://www .sfchronicle.com/bayarea/article/When-an-outlaw-s-severed -head-went-on-tour-in-SF-12277208.php.

Library of Congress. "Gold!" Today in History-January 24. Retrieved February 9, 2018. https://www.loc.gov/item /today-in-history/january-24.

Newsela. "Primary Sources: Life at a Mining Camp During the California Gold Rush." Newsela, October 30, 2016. https:// newsela.com/read/primary-source-life-at-mining-camp /id/21912/quiz/0.

Nichols, Catherine. "The Good Guy/Bad Guy Myth." Aeon, January 25, 2018. https://aeon.co/essays/why-is-pop-culture -obsessed-with-battles-between-good-and-evil.

Our Documents. "Treaty of Guadalupe Hidalgo." Retrieved February 9, 2018. https://www.ourdocuments.gov/doc .php?flash=true&doc=26.

Paz, Ireneo. *Viva Y Aventuras Del Mas Celebre Bandido Sonorense Joaquín Murrieta: Sus Grandes Proezas en California*. Houston, TX: Arte Público Press, University of Houston, 1999.

INDEX

P

Pico, Andrés, 25
Polk, James, 8, 38

R

revenge, 15–17, 19, 34
Ridge, John Rollins, 18
Robin Hood of El Dorado, The, 18, 32

S

Sacramento Valley, 7
Sonora, 4, 12, 13, 26, 31
Sutter, John, 7

T

Treaty of Guadalupe Hidalgo, 10–12

V

Valenzuela, Joaquín, 15, 25, 29

ABOUT THE AUTHOR

Avery Elizabeth Hurt is the author of many books for children and young adults. She is not sure how much of the story of Joaquín Murrieta is true, but she loved digging around for bits and pieces of the story. She very much hopes that he was a real hero and not a villain.

PHOTO CREDITS